PITY THE BEAUTIFUL

ALSO BY DANA GIOIA

POETRY

Daily Horoscope
The Gods of Winter
Interrogations at Noon

CRITICAL COLLECTIONS

Can Poetry Matter?: Essays on Poetry and American Culture
The Barrier of a Common Language:
Essays on Contemporary British Poetry
Disappearing Ink: Poetry at the End of Print Culture

TRANSLATIONS

Mottetti: Poems of Love by Eugenio Montale
The Madness of Hercules by Seneca

OPERA LIBRETTI

Nosferatu
Tony Caruso's Final Broadcast

PITY THE
BEAUTIFUL

. . .

POEMS BY

Dana Gioia

Graywolf Press

This publication is made possible in part by a grant provided by the
Minnesota State Arts Board, through an appropriation by the
Minnesota State Legislature from the Minnesota general fund and
its arts and cultural heritage fund with money from the vote of
the people of Minnesota on November 4, 2008, and a grant from the
Wells Fargo Foundation Minnesota. Significant support has also been
provided by the National Endowment for the Arts; Target;
the McKnight Foundation; and other generous contributions from
foundations, corporations, and individuals. To these organizations
and individuals we offer our heartfelt thanks.

Published by Graywolf Press
250 Third Avenue North, Suite 600
Minneapolis, Minnesota 55401

www.graywolfpress.org

Published in the United States of America

ISBN 978-1-55597-613-2

2 4 6 8 9 7 5 3 1
First Graywolf Printing, 2012

Library of Congress Control Number: 2012932783

Cover design: Jeenee Lee Design

Cover photograph: Eric Lindbloom Photography,
Angel, S. Miniato, Florence

For Morten Lauridsen

The necessary angel

CONTENTS

I.

THE PRESENT / 3

THE ANGEL WITH THE BROKEN WING / 4

PROPHECY / 6

REUNION / 8

THE ROAD / 9

SHOPPING / 10

THE LUNATIC, THE LOVER, AND THE POET / 13

II.

PRAYER AT WINTER SOLSTICE / 17

FINDING A BOX OF FAMILY LETTERS / 18

THE FREEWAYS CONSIDERED AS EARTH GODS / 20

LAS ANIMAS (LUZI) / 22

HUNT *(LUZI)* / 24

THE SEVEN DEADLY SINS / 26

AUTUMN INAUGURAL / 27

SPECIAL TREATMENTS WARD / 29

III.

HAUNTED / 35

IV. Words for Music

PITY THE BEAUTIFUL / 45
THE HEART OF THE MATTER / 46
COLD SAN FRANCISCO / 47
FOUR SONGS FROM
TONY CARUSO'S FINAL BROADCAST
1. Marketing Department Trio / 48
2. Maria Callas's Aria / 50
3. Tony's Last Aria / 52
4. Final Duet / 53

V.

THE APPLE ORCHARD / 57
ON THE SHORE *(LUZI)* / 58
BEING HAPPY / 59
THE COAT / 60
THE ARGUMENT / 61
MY LOVE, DON'T BELIEVE *(CATTAFI)* / 62
THESE LITTLE BIRDS *(CATTAFI)* / 63
AFTER A LINE OF NERUDA / 64
WHO'S THERE? / 65
STARTING OVER / 66
MAJORITY / 68

NOTES ON THE POEMS / 71

PITY THE BEAUTIFUL

· I ·

caminante, no hay camino
se hace camino al andar.

traveler, there is no road,
the road is made by walking.

—ANTONIO MACHADO

THE PRESENT

The present that you gave me months ago
is still unopened by our bed,
sealed in its rich blue paper and bright bow.
I've even left the card unread
and kept the ribbon knotted tight.
Why needlessly unfold and bring to light
the elegant contrivances that hide
the costly secret waiting still inside?

THE ANGEL WITH THE BROKEN WING

I am the Angel with the Broken Wing,
The one large statue in this quiet room.
The staff finds me too fierce, and so they shut
Faith's ardor in this air-conditioned tomb.

The docents praise my elegant design
Above the chatter of the gallery.
Perhaps I am a masterpiece of sorts—
The perfect emblem of futility.

Mendoza carved me for a country church.
(His name's forgotten now except by me.)
I stood beside a gilded altar where
The hopeless offered God their misery.

I heard their women whispering at my feet—
Prayers for the lost, the dying, and the dead.
Their candles stretched my shadow up the wall,
And I became the hunger that they fed.

I broke my left wing in the Revolution
(Even a saint can savor irony)
When troops were sent to vandalize the chapel.
They hit me once—almost apologetically.

For even the godless feel something in a church,
A twinge of hope, fear? Who knows what it is?
A trembling unaccounted by their laws,
An ancient memory they can't dismiss.

There are so many things I must tell God!
The howling of the damned can't reach so high.
But I stand like a dead thing nailed to a perch,
A crippled saint against a painted sky.

PROPHECY

Sometimes a child will stare out of a window
for a moment or an hour—deciphering
the future from a dusky summer sky.

Does he imagine that some wisp of cloud
reveals the signature of things to come?
Or that the world's a book we learn to translate?

And sometimes a girl stands naked by a mirror
imagining beauty in a stranger's eyes
finding a place where fear leads to desire.

For what is prophecy but the first inkling
of what we ourselves must call into being?
The call need not be large. No voice in thunder.

It's not so much what's spoken as what's heard—
and recognized, of course. The gift is listening
and hearing what is only meant for you.

Life has its mysteries, annunciations,
and some must wear a crown of thorns. I found
my Via Dolorosa in your love.

And sometimes we proceed by prophecy,
or not at all—even if only to know
what destiny requires us to renounce.

O Lord of indirection and ellipses,
ignore our prayers. Deliver us from distraction.
Slow our heartbeat to a cricket's call.

In the green torpor of the afternoon,
bless us with ennui and quietude.
And grant us only what we fear, so that

Underneath the murmur of the wasp
we hear the dry grass bending in the wind
and the spider's silken whisper from its web.

REUNION

This is my past where no one knows me.
These are my friends whom I can't name—
Here in a field where no one chose me,
The faces older, the voices the same.

Why does this stranger rise to greet me?
What is the joke that makes him smile,
As he calls the children together to meet me
Bringing them forward in single file?

I nod pretending to recognize them,
Not knowing exactly what I should say.
Why does my presence seem to surprise them?
Who is the woman who turns away?

Is this my home or an illusion?
The bread on the table smells achingly real.
Must I at last solve my confusion,
Or is confusion all I can feel?

THE ROAD

He sometimes felt that he had missed his life
By being far too busy looking for it.
Searching the distance, he often turned to find
That he had passed some milestone unaware,
And someone else was walking next to him,
First friends, then lovers, now children and a wife.
They were good company—generous, kind,
But equally bewildered to be there.

He noticed then that no one chose the way—
All seemed to drift by some collective will.
The path grew easier with each passing day,
Since it was worn and mostly sloped downhill.
The road ahead seemed hazy in the gloom.
Where was it he had meant to go, and with whom?

SHOPPING

I enter the temple of my people but do not pray.
I pass the altars of the gods but do not kneel
Or offer sacrifices proper to the season.

Strolling the hushed aisles of the department store,
I see visions shining under glass,
Divinities of leather, gold, and porcelain,
Shrines of cut crystal, stainless steel, and silicon.

But I wander the arcades of abundance,
Empty of desire, no credit to my people,
Envying the acolytes their passionate faith.
Blessed are the acquisitive,
For theirs is the kingdom of commerce.

Redeem me, gods of the mall and marketplace.
Mercury, protector of cell phones and fax machines,
Venus, patroness of bath and bedroom chains,
Tantalus, guardian of the food court.

Beguile me with the aromas of coffee, musk, and cinnamon.
Surround me with delicately colored soaps and moisturizing creams.
Comfort me with posters of children with perfect smiles
And pouting teenage models clad in lingerie.
I am not made of stone.

Show me satins, linen, crêpe de chine, and silk,
Heaped like cumuli in the morning sky,
As if all caravans and argosies ended in this parking lot
To fill these stockrooms and loading docks.

Sing me the hymns of no cash down and the installment plan,
Of custom fit, remote control, and priced to move.
Whisper the blessing of Egyptian cotton, polyester, and cashmere.
Tell me in what department my desire shall be found.

Because I would buy happiness if I could find it,
Spend all that I possessed or could borrow.
But what can I bring you from these sad emporia?
Where in this splendid clutter
Shall I discover the one true thing?

Nothing to carry, I should stroll easily
Among the crowded countertops and eager cashiers,
Bypassing the sullen lines and footsore customers,
Spending only my time, discounting all I see.

Instead I look for you among the pressing crowds,
But they know nothing of you, turning away,
Carrying their brightly packaged burdens.
There is no angel among the vending stalls and signage.

Where are you, my fugitive? Without you
There is nothing but the getting and the spending
Of things that have a price.
Why else have I stalked the leased arcades
Searching the kiosks and the cash machines?

Where are you, my errant soul and innermost companion?
Are you outside amid the potted palm trees,
Bumming a cigarette or joking with the guards,
Or are you wandering the parking lot
Lost among the rows of Subarus and Audis?

Or is it you I catch a sudden glimpse of
Smiling behind the greasy window of the bus
As it disappears into the evening rush?

THE LUNATIC, THE LOVER,
AND THE POET

The tales we tell are either false or true,
But neither purpose is the point. We weave
The fabric of our own existence out of words,
And the right story tells us who we are.
Perhaps it is the words that summon us.
The tale is often wiser than the teller.
There is no naked truth but what we wear.

So let me bring this story to our bed.
The world, I say, depends upon a spell
Spoken each night by lovers unaware
Of their own sorcery. In innocence
Or agony the same words must be said,
Or the raging moon will darken in the sky.
The night grow still. The winds of dawn expire.

And if I'm wrong, it cannot be by much.
We know our own existence came from touch,
The new soul summoned into life by lust.
And love's shy tongue awakens in such fire—
Flesh against flesh and midnight whispering—
As if the only purpose of desire
Were to express its infinite unfolding.

And so, my love, we are two lunatics,
Secretaries to the wordless moon,
Lying awake, together or apart,
Transcribing every touch or aching absence
Into our endless, intimate palaver,
Body to body, naked to the night,
Appareled only in our utterance.

· II ·

How with this rage shall beauty hold a plea?

—WILLIAM SHAKESPEARE

PRAYER AT WINTER SOLSTICE

Blessed is the road that keeps us homeless.
Blessed is the mountain that blocks our way.

Blessed are hunger and thirst, loneliness and all forms of desire.
Blessed is the labor that exhausts us without end.

Blessed are the night and the darkness that blinds us.
Blessed is the cold that teaches us to feel.

Blessed are the cat, the child, the cricket, and the crow.
Blessed is the hawk devouring the hare.

Blessed are the saint and the sinner who redeem each other.
Blessed are the dead, calm in their perfection.

Blessed is the pain that humbles us.
Blessed is the distance that bars our joy.

Blessed is this shortest day that makes us long for light.
Blessed is the love that in losing we discover.

FINDING A BOX OF FAMILY LETTERS

The dead say little in their letters
they haven't said before.
We find no secrets, and yet
how different every sentence sounds
heard across the years.

My father breaks my heart
simply by being so young and handsome.
He's half my age, with jet-black hair.
Look at him in his navy uniform
grinning beside his dive-bomber.

Come back, Dad! I want to shout.
He says he misses all of us
(though I haven't yet been born).
He writes from places I never knew he saw,
and everyone he mentions now is dead.

There is a large, long photograph
curled like a diploma—a banquet sixty years ago.
My parents sit uncomfortably
among tables of dark-suited strangers.
The mildewed paper reeks of regret.

I wonder what song the band was playing,
just out of frame, as the photographer
arranged your smiles. A waltz? A foxtrot?
Get out there on the floor and dance!
You don't have forever.

What does it cost to send a postcard
to the underworld? I'll buy
a penny stamp from World War II
and mail it downtown at the old post office
just as the courthouse clock strikes twelve.

Surely the ghost of some postal worker
still makes his nightly rounds, his routine
too tedious for him to notice when it ended.
He works so slowly he moves back in time
carrying our dead letters to their lost addresses.

It's silly to get sentimental.
The dead have moved on. So should we.
But isn't it equally simpleminded to miss
the special expertise of the departed
in clarifying our long-term plans?

They never let us forget that the line
between them and us is only temporary.
Get out there and dance! the letters shout
adding, *Love always. Can't wait to get home!*
And soon we will be. *See you there.*

THE FREEWAYS CONSIDERED
AS EARTH GODS

These are the gods who rule the golden land.
Their massive bodies stretch across the countryside,
Filling the valleys, climbing the hills, curving along the coast,
Crushing the earth from which they draw their sustenance
Of tar and concrete, asphalt, sand, and steel.

They are not new, these most ancient of divinities.
Our clamor woke them from the subdivided soil.
They rise to rule us, neither cruel nor kind,
But indifferent to our ephemeral humanity.
Their motives are unknowable and profound.

The gods do not condescend to our frailty.
They cleave our cities, push aside our homes,
Provide no place to walk or rest or gather.
The pathways of the gods are empty, flat, and hard.
They draw us to them, filling us with longing.

We do not fail to worship them. Each morning
Millions creep in slow procession on our pilgrimages.
We crave the dangerous power of their presence.
And they demand blood sacrifice, so we mount
Our daily holocaust on the blackened ground.

The gods command the hilltops and the valleys.
They rule the deserts and the howling wilderness.
They drink the rivers and clear the mountains in their way.
They consume the earth and the increase of the field.
They burn the air with their rage.

We are small. We are weak. We are mortal.
Ten thousand of us could not move one titan's arm.
We need their strength and speed.
We bend to their justice and authority.
These are the gods of California. Worship them.

LAS ANIMAS

Fire everywhere, soft fire of brushwood, fire
on walls where a faint shadow flickers
but lacks the strength to imprint itself, fire
in the distance rising and falling across the hills
like a bright thread through the spreading ashes,
fire in flakes from the trellised vines and branches.

Here neither before nor after its proper time,
but now that everything in this festive,
sad valley exhausts its life, exhausts its fire,
I turn back and count my dead,
and their procession seems longer, trembling
leaf by leaf from the first felled tree.

Grant them peace, eternal peace, carry them
to safety—far from this whirlwind
of ash and flame that twists choking
through the ravines, wandering the paths,
spinning aimlessly, then disappears.
Let death be only death, nothing other
than death, beyond struggle, beyond life.
Grant them peace, eternal peace, appease them.

Down there where the harvest is thicker,
they plow, they roll their barrels to the spring,
they whisper in the quiet transformations
of each hour. A young dog stretches out
in the corner of the garden for a nap.

A fire this gentle is barely enough, perhaps
not even enough, to cast light long
on this life's undergrowth. Only another fire
can do the rest and then more—
to consume these remains, to change
them into light, clear and incorruptible.

Requiems from the dead for the living, requiems
in each flame for the living and the dead.
Stir the embers: night is here, the night
that spreads its pulsing web between the mountains,
now the eyes fail, but from the heat,
from the darkness, they know what remains.

(From the Italian of Mario Luzi)

HUNT

The ashen sea rushing against the steep-walled bunker,
the long-awaited flocks of birds passing or returning,
screeching more now than ever, screeching: "It is autumn,
it is the time of your birth into this life," just as one by one
they fall to the bullets, still trying to take flight as they fall,
and as far as the eye can see, branch by branch
the forest is losing its leaves, and fringed in fire
lie shattered lives, feathers still throbbing.

Here and now, where a dog startles a partridge,
where sometimes gypsy kings encamp
to rest a few hours on the journey
from town to town, where leaves and birds,
both native and migratory, light and heavy,
fall to the ground which is wet
but not yet cold, it is the time
of my birth, the time and place together
to remember my murdered dead,
my fallen ones lost under fire—not long ago
my fathers fell, soon my brothers—
the wind of life, the wind of plunder
and of death, strikes me full in the face,
cutting off my breath, but I,
still craving food, raise my hands
into the trees and pluck the fruit.

"It is the time of your birth." They rest,
they die, surrounded by life, they perish
in time to come; and the joyful ones, the dark ones
spread out over the dead leaves, over the wings
lifeless as lead to conquer and atone
for all things which have an end.

(From the Italian of Mario Luzi)

THE SEVEN DEADLY SINS

Forget about the other six, says Pride.
They're only using you.
Admittedly, Lust is a looker,
but you can do better.

And why do they keep bringing us
to this cheesy dive?
The food's so bad that even Gluttony
can't finish his meal.

Notice how Avarice
keeps refilling his glass
whenever he thinks we're not looking,
while Envy eyes your plate.

Hell, we're not even done, and Anger
is already arguing about the bill.
I'm the only one who
ever leaves a decent tip.

Let them all go, the losers!
It's a relief to see Sloth's
fat ass go out the door.
But stick around. I have a story

that not everyone appreciates—
about the special satisfaction
of staying on board as the last
grubby lifeboat pushes away.

AUTUMN INAUGURAL

I.

There will always be those who reject ceremony,
Who claim that resolution requires no fanfare,
Those who demand the spirit stay fixed
Like a desert saint, fed only on faith,
To worship in no temple but the weather.

There will always be the austere ones
Who mount denial's shaky ladder
To drape the statues or whitewash the frescoed wall,
As if the still star of painted plaster
Praised creation less then the evening's original.

And they are right. Symbols betray us.
They are always more or less than what
Is really meant. But shall there be no
Processions by torchlight because we are weak?
What native speech do we share but imperfection?

II.

Praise to the rituals that celebrate change,
Old robes worn for new beginnings,
Solemn protocol where the mutable soul,
Surrounded by ancient experience, grows
Young in the imagination's white dress.

Because it is not the rituals we honor
But our trust in what they signify, these rites
That honor us as witnesses—whether to watch
Lovers swear loyalty in a careless world
Or a newborn washed with water and oil.

So praise to innocence—impulsive and evergreen—
And let the old be touched by youth's
Wayward astonishment at learning something new,
And dream of a future so fitting and so just
That our desire will bring it into being.

SPECIAL TREATMENTS WARD

I.

So this is where the children come to die,
hidden on the hospital's highest floor.
They wear their bandages like uniforms
and pull their IV rigs along the hall
with slow and careful steps. Or bald and pale,
they lie in bright pajamas on their beds,
watching another world on a screen.

The mothers spend their nights inside the ward,
sleeping on chairs that fold out into beds,
too small to lie in comfort. Soon they slip
beside their children, as if they might mesh
those small bruised bodies back into their flesh.
Instinctively they feel that love so strong
protects a child. Each morning proves them wrong.

No one chooses to be here. We play the parts
that we are given—horrible as they are.
We try to play them well, whatever that means.
We need to talk, though talking breaks our hearts.
The doctors come and go like oracles,
their manner cool, omniscient, and oblique.
There is a word that no one ever speaks.

II.

I put this poem aside twelve years ago
because I could not bear remembering
the faces it evoked, and every line
seemed—still seems—so inadequate and grim.

What right had I whose son had walked away
to speak for those who died? And I'll admit
I wanted to forget. I'd lost one child
and couldn't bear to watch another die.

Not just the silent boy who shared our room,
but even the bird-thin figures dimly glimpsed
shuffling deliberately, disjointedly
like ancient soldiers after a parade.

Whatever strength the task required I lacked.
No well-stitched words could suture shut these wounds.
And so I stopped . . .
But there are poems we do not choose to write.

III.

The children visit me, not just in dream,
appearing suddenly, silently—
insistent, unprovoked, unwelcome.

They've taken off their milky bandages
to show the raw, red lesions they still bear.
Risen they are healed but not made whole.

A few I recognize, untouched by years.
I cannot name them—their faces pale and gray
like ashes fallen from a distant fire.

What use am I to them, almost a stranger?
I cannot wake them from their satin beds.
Why do they seek me? They never speak.

And vagrant sorrow cannot bless the dead.

· III ·

And the lovers lie abed
With all their griefs in their arms.

—DYLAN THOMAS

HAUNTED

"I don't believe in ghosts," he said. "Such nonsense.
But years ago I actually saw one."
He seemed quite serious, and so I asked.

It happened almost forty years ago.
The world was different then—not just for ghosts—
slower, less frantic. You're too young to know
life without cell phones, laptops, satellite.
You didn't bring the world with you everywhere.
Out in the country, you were quite alone.

I was in love with Mara then, if love
is the right word for that particular
delusion. We were young. We thought we could
create a life made only of peak moments.
We laughed. We drank. We argued and made love.
Our battles were Homeric—not Homer's heroes
but his gods, petty, arrogant Olympians
thundering in their egotistic rage.

Mara was brilliant, beautiful, refined.
She'd walk into a room dressed for the evening,
and I would lose a breath. She seemed to shine
as movie stars shine, made only of light.
And did I mention she was rich? And cruel?

Do you know what it's like to be in love
with someone bad? Not simply bad for you,
but slightly evil? You have to decide
either to be the victim or accomplice.
I'm not the victim type. That's what she liked.

I envied her sublime self-confidence.
She could freeze someone with a single sentence,
too witty to be rude but deeply wounding,
impossible to deflect or forget.
If I sound slightly bitter, please understand,
it is myself I now despise, not Mara.
She simply recognized what I desired.

Her uncle owned a house up in the Berkshires,
not just a summer house, a country manor,
three stories high with attics, basement, turrets,
surrounded by great lawns and sunken gardens,
hundreds of wooded acres whispering wealth.

We came up for a few days in late autumn,
driving through bare woods under a gray sky,
the landscape still, no birds, barely a breeze,
hushed as the hour after heavy snowfall.

The house had been vacated since September.
I had imagined it as dark and gothic,
cloaked in shadow like something out of Lovecraft,
but the decor was opulently cozy,
a proper refuge for a Robber Baron,
stuffed with *objets* to certify his status,
though slightly shabby from a century's use.

The art was grand, authentic, second rate.
Florentine bronzes, Belgian tapestries,
carved stonework pried from bankrupt Tudor manors,
and landscapes by the minor Barbizons.
Nothing quite fit together. I suspect

sumptuous excess was the desired effect,
a joyful shout to celebrate success—
good taste be damned—let's just indulge ourselves
and revel like a child who greets his playmates
by emptying his toy chest on the floor.
What fun is wealth if no one notices?
Mara seemed to think so. What did I know?
I'd never seen the rich up close before.

While Mara showered, I explored the cellars,
searching a maze of mildewed storage rooms
until I found a faux medieval door,
flanked by a pair of somber wooden saints.
You should have seen the wine her uncle owned—
six vaulted rooms stocked with the great estates,
bin after bin of legendary names,
Château Margaux, Latour, Lafite Rothschild,
a prodigal accumulation formed
on such a scale he could have entertained
Napoleon and half his *Grande Armée*.

I chose two bottles of prewar Pétrus
that probably cost as much as my month's rent.
Clutching their dusty necks, I closed the door,
and told the saints, "I could get used to this."
They didn't condescend to give an answer.

That night we drank in the high paneled library,
a great inferno blazing in the fireplace.
Naked Diana stood in tapestry
above us on the wall. Below her, Mara,
stylishly overdressed, refilled our glasses.

Resplendently the room reminded us
that beauty always bears a heavy price.
White tiger skins lay stretched across the floor.
Martyred Sebastian twisted on a pedestal.
Even the dusty books were bound in leather.

Mara loved having me as audience.
She sat there, half illumined by the fire
and half in shadow, spinning out long stories.
They were as fine as anything in books.
No, they were better because they were true.

She was a connoisseur of *Schadenfreude*
and was especially wicked in describing
her former lovers—imitating them,
cataloguing their signature stupidities,
and relishing their subsequent misfortunes.
(I'm surely in her repertory now.)

At first I was embarrassed by her candor.
I felt more like a confidant than lover,
but gradually I understood the motive—
even she needed someone to impress.
Life was a contest. Mara was a champion.
What good was winning if no one noticed?

Of course, that night we drank too much and argued.
She strode off, slamming doors theatrically.
I sat still, slowly finishing my drink,
feigning indifference—just as she would have—
and then went to the other wing to sleep.
Let her find me, I thought. Let her apologize.
She won't like sleeping in this house alone.

The room was cold, and I was too annoyed
to fall asleep. I stretched out on the bed,
still wearing all my clothes, and tried to read.
Believe it or not, the book was Shakespeare's sonnets.
What sweeter text for wounded vanity?
Farewell, thou art too dear for my possessing.
I'd found an old edition in the library,
and from sheer spitefulness I'd stolen it.
That night each poem seemed written just for me.
What is your substance, whereof are you made,
That millions of strange shadows on you tend?

I hope this explanation makes it clear
I wasn't sleeping when I saw her enter—
Mara, I thought, mad at being ignored,
coming to make a scene. But, no, it was
a handsome woman in her early forties.
I thought she might have been a housekeeper
come in from town to check up on the place,
but why was she so elegantly dressed?

I started to explain why I was there.
She didn't seem to hear and turned away.
Could she be deaf? I didn't want to scare her.
Something was wrong. I couldn't see her clearly.
She seemed at once herself and her own reflection
shimmering on the surface of clear water
where fleeting shadows twisted in the depths.

I found it hard admitting what I saw.
She seemed to be a ghost, though that sounds crazy.
Oddly, I wasn't scared—just full of wonder,
watching this thing I knew could not exist,

this woman standing by her dressing table,
translucent, insubstantial, but still there,
and utterly oblivious of me.
First to be haunted, then to be ignored!

Her back toward me, she started to undress.
Now I was panicked and embarrassed both.
I spoke much louder. She made no response.
Now wearing only a long silk chemise,
she turned toward me, still strangely indistinct,
the fabric undulating, as if alive.
I felt her eyes appraise me, and I sat
half paralyzed as she approached the bed.

Here I was face to face with a dead soul,
some entity regathered from the dust,
returned like Lazarus from the silent tomb,
whose mere existence, right before my eyes,
confounded my belief there could not be
an afterlife. Think what this meeting represented—
a skeptic witnessing the unexplained.

I could have learned the secrets of the dead
if there are any secrets, which I doubt.
So how did I address this revenant,
this traveler from the undiscovered country,
who stared at me with dark, unblinking eyes?
I caught my breath, got on my feet, and said—
nothing at all. The words stuck in my throat.

We stood there face to face, inches apart.
Her pale skin shined like a window catching sunlight,
both bright and clear, but chilling to the touch.
She stared at me with undisguised contempt,
and then she whispered, almost in a hiss,
"You don't belong here. No, you don't belong here."
She slowly reached to touch me, and I ran
leaving behind both Shakespeare and my shoes.

Mara was still awake when I arrived.
The lamp was on. The fireplace ablaze.
And she stretched naked under satin sheets.
(She couldn't resist striking pinup poses.)
"So, you've come back?" she yawned with mock ennui,
then added with a smirk, "You weren't gone long."
I didn't say a word of what I'd seen.

We used to sleep in one another's arms,
our two slim bodies interlaced like hands.
That night I held her, feeling our hearts beat—
first hers, then mine—always out of sync,
and in the dark I thought, *I don't belong here,*
I don't belong here. Slipping out of bed,
I quickly dressed, and what I couldn't wear
I left behind—the clothes, the books, the camera,
no longer mine. What a surprise to first feel
the liberations of divestiture.

I moved with such new lightness down the stairs,
watched by mute saints and marble goddesses.
Then out the door. I closed it quietly.
The lock clicked shut. Good-bye to both my ghosts.

I made it to the county road by dawn
and hitched a ride on an old dairy truck.
"What happened to your shoes?" the driver said.
"No, better yet, don't tell me. Just get in."

I climbed in, and one road led to another.
And now I'm in your bar. That's probably not
the story you expected from a monk,
delivering brandy from the monastery.
Not all of us began as altar boys.

I've been there fifteen years. I like the drill—
Poverty, Chastity, and Growing Grapes.
The archbishop calls my port a miracle.
Don't tell His Grace, but I still doubt there is
an afterlife. That's not why I stay there.
This is the life I didn't want to waste.

· IV ·

WORDS FOR MUSIC

Cold dark deep and absolutely clear

—ELIZABETH BISHOP

PITY THE BEAUTIFUL

Pity the beautiful,
the dolls, and the dishes,
the babes with big daddies
granting their wishes.

Pity the pretty boys,
the hunks, and Apollos,
the golden lads whom
success always follows.

The hotties, the knock-outs,
the tens out of ten,
the drop-dead gorgeous,
the great leading men.

Pity the faded,
the bloated, the blowsy,
the paunchy Adonis
whose luck's gone lousy.

Pity the gods,
no longer divine.
Pity the night
the stars lose their shine.

THE HEART OF THE MATTER

The heart of the matter, the ghost of a chance,
A tremor, a fever, an ache in the chest.
The moth and the candle beginning their dance,
A cool white sheet on which nothing will rest.

Come sit beside me. I've waited alone.
What you need to confess I already know.
The scent of your shame is a heavy cologne
That lingers for hours after you go.

The dregs of the bottle, the end of the line,
The laggard, the loser, the last one to know.
The unfinished book, the dead-end sign,
And last summer's garden buried in snow.

COLD SAN FRANCISCO

I shall meet you again in cold San Francisco
On the hillside street overlooking the bay.
We shall go to the house where we buried the years,
Where the door is locked, and we haven't a key.
We'll pause on the steps as the fog burns away,
And the chill waves shimmer in the sun's dim glow,
And we'll gaze down the hill at the bustling piers
Where the gulls shout their hymns to being alive,
And the high-masted boats that we never sailed
Stand poised to explore the innocent blue.
I shall speak your name like a foreign word,
Uncertain what it means, and you—
What will you say in that salt-heavy air
On that bright afternoon that will never arrive?

FOUR SONGS FROM
TONY CARUSO'S FINAL BROADCAST

I. MARKETING DEPARTMENT TRIO

Classical music's
Gotta go.
All the surveys
Tell us so.
Brahms is boring.
Bach is dreary.
Morning drive time
Should be cheery.

Grieg is stale.
Mozart moldy.
Give us this day
Our golden oldie.
Tchaikovsky's pathetic.
Schubert's a nerd.
And once is too much
For Beethoven's Third.

The past is over.
Let's clean house.
Out with Verdi.
Good-bye Strauss.
Curtains for opera.
Unstring that cello.
Make the music
Soft and mellow.

Whether you're driving
Or trying to score,
Lean back, relax,
While our ratings soar.
Mile after mile
Commute with a smile.
So bye-bye Beethoven,
And don't touch that dial!

2. MARIA CALLAS'S ARIA

I. *Cavatina*

I have not come for you.
I come here to perform,
To show you what you might have been.
I'm nothing but the role I play—
Nothing and everything.

They claim that my career was short.
You know it was the longest ever.
No other singer burned as hot,
As brightly, or as long as I—
Nothing and everything.

You understand what critics don't.
They call us stars because we burn
In darkness—cold, remote, and bright,
Unreachable, unaging—
Nothing and everything!

II. *Cabaletta*

To be divine
A woman must die,
Offer her flesh
To satisfy
A freezing fire,
Fed and sustained
By pure desire,
That burns so bright
It fills the sky.

To be divine
A woman must die,
Seeking the pain
To magnify
A sacrifice
That makes her seem
Both fire and ice,
A star to pierce
The darkest sky.

3. TONY'S LAST ARIA

Memories of love are midnight's poison,
The slow venom that will not kill,
The drink that renders thirst unending,
Drawn from the rivers of hell.

Memories of loss are midnight's passion,
The cross it carries to the bone-covered hill,
The pain that offers no redemption,
But the slow descent to hell.

Memories of love are midnight's prison.
The heart's dark inescapable cell.
Tear off the lock, pull down the walls,
You still remain in hell.

4. FINAL DUET

Only us and only now.
Beyond the dark, beyond desire—
The song we make together.

Love requires only one
Reciprocate its melody
Two dreamers locked in unison.

Only us and only now,
Nothing else that we desire
Beyond the song we make together.

Love and darkness now are one.
Sleep in my arms and you will find
Ecstasy in oblivion.

Only us and only now
Lost in the sleep we both desire
In the night we share together—

This night we sing together.

· V ·

This luscious and impeccable fruit of life

—WALLACE STEVENS

THE APPLE ORCHARD

You won't remember it—the apple orchard
We wandered through one April afternoon,
Climbing the hill behind the empty farm.

A city boy, I'd never seen a grove
Burst in full flower or breathed the bittersweet
Perfume of blossoms mingled with the dust.

A quarter mile of trees in fragrant rows
Arching above us. We walked the aisle,
Alone in spring's ephemeral cathedral.

We had the luck, if you can call it that,
Of having been in love but never lovers—
The bright flame burning, fed by pure desire.

Nothing consumed, such secrets brought to light!
There was a moment when I stood behind you,
Reached out to spin you toward me . . . but I stopped.

What more could I have wanted from that day?
Everything, of course. Perhaps that was the point—
To learn that what we will not grasp is lost.

ON THE SHORE

The waves unbend beneath the empty wharves,
And the old storm god departs exhausted.
What are you doing? Me, I fill a lantern,
Cleaning the room in which I find myself
With neither news of you nor those you love.

Our scattered company collects itself.
After such storms, we count up the survivors.
But where are you? Safe in some port, I hope . . .
The lighthouse keeper rows out in his skiff,
Checking for damage, eyeing the horizon.
Time and the sea afford us such small pauses.

(From the Italian of Mario Luzi)

BEING HAPPY

Of course it was doomed. I know that now,
but it ended so quickly, and I was young.
I hardly remember that summer in Seattle—
except for her. The city seems just a rainy backdrop.
From the moment I first saw her at the office
I was hooked. I started visiting her floor.

I couldn't work unless I caught a glimpse of her.
Once we exchanged glances, but we never spoke.
Then at a party we found ourselves alone.
We started kissing and ended up in bed.
We talked all night. She claimed she had liked me
secretly for months. I wonder now if that was true.

Two weeks later her father had a heart attack.
While she was in Chicago, they shut down our division.
I was never one for writing letters.
On the phone we had less to say each time.
And that was it—just those two breathless weeks,
then years of mild regret and intermittent speculation.

Being happy is mostly like that. You don't see it up close.
You recognize it later from the ache of memory.
And you can't recapture it. You only get to choose
whether to remember or forget, whether to feel remorse
or nothing at all. Maybe it wasn't really love.
But who can tell when nothing deeper ever came along?

THE COAT

I saw someone wearing your coat today,
The sleek, short pink one you bought in L.A.
I never liked it much—too bright, too retro—
But you brought it off. You always do.

I followed the woman down the icy street
Until she disappeared into the Metro.
Only then I realized I hadn't seen her face,
Except to register she wasn't you.

I thought of her traveling underground
To Shady Grove or Rockville Meadows,
Bearing away this relic of your grace,
A pink Persephone among pin-striped shadows.

Why had your ghost returned here with this warning?
Was it only to flaunt her power to flee?
Or had the coat itself come simply to taunt me
With the fragrance of spring on a cold, dead morning?

THE ARGUMENT

After you put the phone down,
The words don't vanish all at once.
They linger in the wires and circuitry,
Pushing their way through the noisy
Crowds of other conversations,
Still trying to provoke a response.

Endlessly repeating themselves,
They want to argue out
Their side of things—furious
That not one syllable will listen.

So angry they hardly notice
How much weaker they become
Each time they speak.
Until at last they huddle
As whispers in the long
Black tunnel of their saying.

But see how strong they are today.
Listen to them rage above the quiet road,
Screeching out their righteousness
Along the miles of tight-strung wire.

MY LOVE, DON'T BELIEVE

My love, don't believe that today
the planet travels on another orbit,
it is the same journey between old
pale stations,
there is always a sparrow flitting
in the flowerbeds
a thought grown stubborn in the mind.
Time turns on the face of the clock, it joins
a trace of fog above the pine trees
the world veers into the regions of cold.
Here are the crumbs on the earth,
the embers in the fireplace,
the wings,
the low and busy hands.

(From the Italian of Bartolo Cattafi)

THESE LITTLE BIRDS

These little birds
would like to hunt you down
use their claws
to tear away your face
this is their sadness
when they watch you
and lower their yellow eyelids.

(From the Italian of Bartolo Cattafi)

AFTER A LINE OF NERUDA

Desnuda, eres tan simple como una de tus manos

Naked, only naked did I know you.
I, who had clothed you in my longing, now
Was undeceived. Naked in the darkness,
No longer blind.

Naked, we read the living text of skin,
Awakened into knowledge beyond naming,
Trading our newfound secrets silently
From lip to lip.

How strange to strip our lives off like old robes,
Dropped to the floor. Not caring what we'll wear—
Centuries from now—when a new sun
Clothes us in light.

But naked in the night, we knew that we
Were flesh and nothing more. There was only *now,*
And our fingers shone brighter than the dawn
That made us part.

WHO'S THERE?

The morning light seems cold and tarnished
rubbing against the curtains
it is too weak to ruffle.

The quiet rooms, the furniture
that someone else picked out, the coffee
left congealing in a cup.

The reading lamp leans forward
intent on telling something
it can't put into words.

No message on the telephone,
the bed empty, the mirror blank,
just a few bills and a statement from the bank.

Who are they addressed to?
Maybe the answer is hidden in the books
waiting in their alphabetical rows.

STARTING OVER

"I'll work harder this time," you reply.
"I know I can start over." Another venture failed.
Another lover gone in bitter recrimination.
The waiter clears the plates. You pour more wine,
your dark eyes gleaming.

Outside the streets fill up. We hear
the low, steady beat of music from the bars,
and the city's unending nocturnal parade—
the lovers, the loners, and the lost,
all eager to touch someone.

You talk of her and her flagrant betrayals.
You lean forward and whisper about your own mistakes.
Tonight your remorse is exquisite and excessive,
the words already polished and refined
by many retellings.

You step outside to light a cigarette.
"I really don't smoke, you know, but sometimes . . ."
You exhale with the studied elegance
of a film noir grifter as you expound
on your future ambitions.

The silken ribbon of your smoke does not rise
but drifts away in slow, suggestive arabesques.
Suggesting what? Perhaps that here
even the wind and air can cultivate
a sensuous lack of purpose.

And you will drift and dissipate like that smoke
in the streets of this beautiful city.
She is the one lover you will not escape.
Each new humiliation and betrayal only rouses you
to more austere devotion.

No drug is more dizzying than love's deception.
And you will trade anything for one
more night in her soft bed. Go. Travel.
Seek your needful redemption. Night will always
bring the old hungers.

You smile with weary but confident charm,
and I commend your virtuous resolution.
The waiter locks the door behind us,
and I watch you vanish into the midnight crowd,
younger every year.

MAJORITY

Now you'd be three,
I said to myself,
seeing a child born
the same summer as you.

Now you'd be six,
or seven, or ten.
I watched you grow
in foreign bodies.

Leaping into a pool, all laughter,
or frowning over a keyboard,
but mostly just standing,
taller each time.

How splendid your most
mundane action seemed
in these joyful proxies.
I often held back tears.

Now you are twenty-one.
Finally, it makes sense
that you have moved away
into your own afterlife.

NOTES ON THE POEMS

The Angel with the Broken Wing

The poem is spoken by a *santo,* a devotional wooden statue carved by a Mexican folk artist.

Las Animas

The title of this poem means "The Souls" in Spanish, specifically the souls of the dead for whom candles are being lit in preparation for the Day of the Dead.

Autumn Inaugural

The season is autumn because the inauguration is academic.

Tony Caruso's Final Broadcast

Tony Caruso's Final Broadcast is a one-act opera written with composer Paul Salerni. The action takes place at a bankrupt classical music radio station on its last night of broadcasting. At midnight the station will convert to an easy-listening format. The station's final show is an opera program hosted by Antonio Caruso, a failed tenor, who has nothing worthwhile left in his life except this program.

Majority

This poem commemorates the twenty-first birthday of my first son who died in infancy.

ACKNOWLEDGMENTS

These poems, often in significantly different versions, have previously appeared in the following journals: *Acumen* (UK), *American Arts Quarterly,* the *American Poetry Review,* the *Dark Horse* (Scotland), *Evansville Review, First Things, Italian Americana,* the *Los Angeles Review, New Criterion,* the *Philadelphia Inquirer, Poet Lore, Virginia Quarterly Review,* and *World Literature Today.*

"The Present," "The Angel with the Broken Wing," "Reunion," "*Las Animas,*" "Hunt," "Special Treatments Ward," "Pity the Beautiful," "My Love, Don't Believe," and "These Little Birds" first appeared in *Poetry.* "Prophecy," "The Lunatic, the Lover, and the Poet," "Autumn Inaugural," "Haunted," "The Heart of the Matter," "The Apple Orchard," and "Being Happy" first appeared in the *Hudson Review.*

The author wishes to thank all of these editors for their generosity and support.

DANA GIOIA was born in Los Angeles in 1950. He received his BA and MBA degrees from Stanford University. He also has an MA in Comparative Literature from Harvard University. For fifteen years he worked as a business executive in New York before quitting in 1992 to write full-time. He has published three earlier collections of poetry—*Daily Horoscope* (1986), *The Gods of Winter* (1991), and *Interrogations at Noon* (2001), which won the American Book Award. Gioia's first critical collection, *Can Poetry Matter?* (1992), was a finalist for the National Book Critics Circle Award. From 2003 to 2009 he served as Chairman of the National Endowment for the Arts. A prolific essayist, reviewer, and translator, Gioia has also published fifteen anthologies of poetry and fiction. He divides his time between Los Angeles and Sonoma County, California. In 2011 he joined the faculty of the University of Southern California as the Judge Widney Professor of Poetry and Public Culture.

This book was based on a design by Tree Swenson. It is set in Galliard type by BookMobile Design and Publishing Services, Minneapolis, Minnesota. Manufactured by Versa Press on acid-free, 30 percent postconsumer wastepaper.